VOCABULARY FROM CLASSICAL ROOTS™

▾ Lee Mountain ▾

5

EDUCATORS PUBLISHING SERVICE
Cambridge and Toronto

Cover photo: Erich Lessing/Art Resource, NY

Printed in the USA

ISBN 978-0-8388-2266-1

22 23 24 25 PPG 22 21 20 19

CONTENTS

PREFACE

Vocabulary from Classical Roots™ encourages you to look at words as members of families. Just as members of a human family usually have things in common, so word families often share similarities. In this book you will get to know groups of words descended from Greek and Latin. These word families are connected to a concept. The concept of "around," for example, is rooted in *circ* from the Latin word *circum.* It is easy to see that such words as *circle, circular,* and *circulation* are members of the *circ* family.

You will notice that most Latin and Greek roots are word parts that usually do not stand alone. But these parts carry meaning. Learning that meaning will help you understand not only the words in this book but also many other words that contain these meaningful parts. For example, when you know that the Latin root *struct* means "to build," you know part of the meaning of *structure, reconstruct,* and *deconstruction.*

This book can do more than increase your recognition of words. It can show you that many words you use today, such as *interrupt* and *astronaut,* have ancestry that can be traced back for centuries. The number of English words descended from Latin and Greek roots is *astronomical,* making them seem almost as numerous as the stars.

NOTES ON USING *VOCABULARY FROM CLASSICAL ROOTS*

1. Latin and Greek forms. The Latin or Greek source of each root or affix appears with its meaning before the definitions of its featured words.

2. Diacritical marks. Following every defined word in *Vocabulary from Classical Roots* is the guide to pronunciation. You will find a key to the diacritical marks used in this book on the inside front cover.

3. Derivation. Information in brackets (after the guide to pronunciation for a word) gives derivations not covered in other lessons. For example, in the lesson on the negative prefix *in-*, after the word *insomnia,* this information appears in brackets: [also derived from Latin *somnus* meaning "sleep"].

4. Familiar Words and Challenge Words. Listed next to groups of defined words are two sets of words belonging to the same family. You probably already know the Familiar Words in the shaded boxes in the margin. Try to figure out the meanings of the Challenge Words, and if you are curious, look them up in a dictionary.

5. Nota Bene. *Nota bene* means "note well" and is usually abbreviated to N.B. In *Vocabulary from Classical Roots,* NOTA BENE will tell you some interesting details about key words or about other words related to the theme of the lesson.

6. Exercises. The exercises help you determine how well you have learned the words while also serving as practice for examinations such as your state and national standardized tests. In each lesson, Exercise A focuses on synonyms or antonyms. Exercise B asks you to use key words to fill in blanks in the context of a passage. Exercise C extends each lesson to include roots and affixes (prefixes and suffixes) related to one of the key words and helps you look at building new words. The review exercises ensure recognition of the meanings of roots and affixes, provide additional opportunities for using featured words in context, and offer writing practice.

LESSON 1

Going in Circles

The root *circ* as in ***circ**le* means "around." The root *cycl* as in *bi**cycl**e* means "revolving" (like the wheels of a bike). In each of the following key words, underline the root.

Key Words

circuit	circulate	cyclone	semicircle
circular	cycle	recycle	unicycle

Using ROOT CLUES

The roots *circ* (around) and *cycl* (revolving) give you clues about meaning. When you spot one of these roots in a word, you have a key to the word's meaning. Use the underlined root clues to help you match the following columns:

1. ______	circulate	A. one revolving wheel
2. ______	unicycle	B. to move around
3. ______	circuit	C. revolving winds
4. ______	cyclone	D. path around which electricity passes

The root clues did not give you complete definitions as the following dictionary listings will. But they got you started by giving you *part* of the meaning. Sometimes that *part* helps you to figure out the word.

CIRC (from the Latin word *circum* meaning "around")

Familiar Words with Root CIRC
- circle
- circus

1. circuit (sər′ kət)

n. A closed route that goes around an object or area, such as the path along which an electric current flows.

Emily put two batteries in the flashlight to complete the circuit.

NOTA BENE

An electrical circuit is seldom *round.* So why does it have the root *circ* as in *circle?* A complete circuit is a path on which all points are connected with no breaks in the line. It is continuous, like the unbroken line of a circle.

Challenge Words with Root CIRC

- circlet
- circuitry
- circuitous

2. circular (sər′ kyə lər)

adj. Having the shape of a circle.

The basketball fell through the circular opening of the hoop and gave our team the lead.

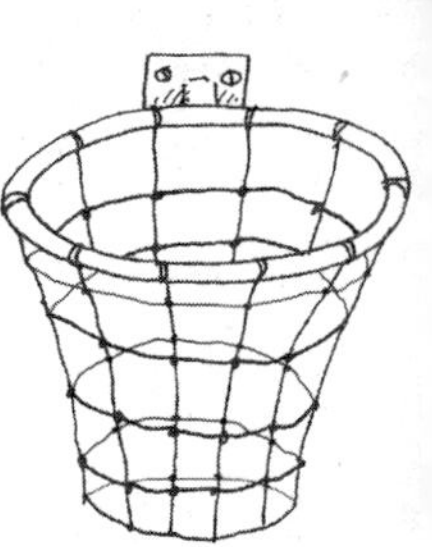

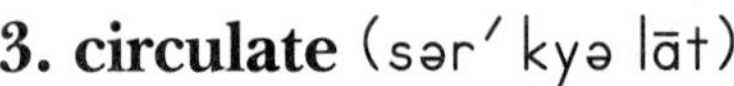

3. circulate (sər′ kyə lāt)

v. 1. To move along a path and return to the same place.

The pumping of the heart makes the blood circulate through the body.

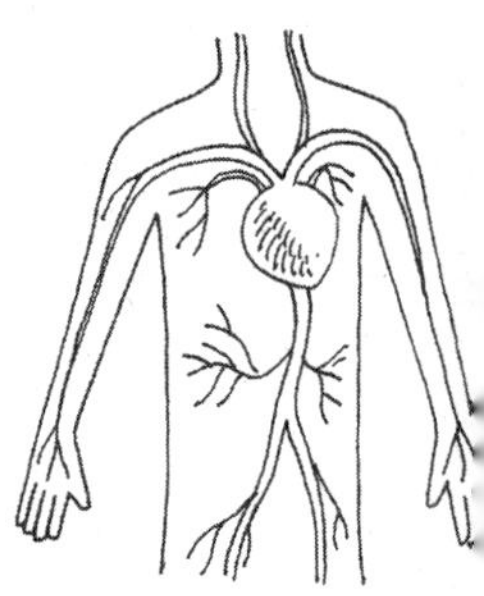

2. To move from person to person or from place to place.

Luis enjoyed meeting new people and often circulated from one group to another at parties.

circulation, n.

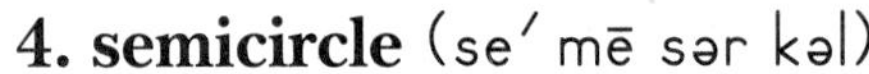

4. semicircle (se′ mē sər kəl)

n. A half circle.

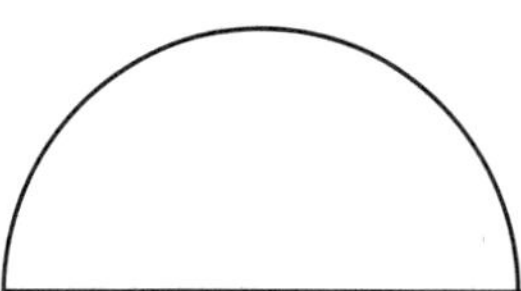

We sat in a semicircle facing the librarian as he explained where to find the books we would need for our reports.

CYCL (from the Greek word *kuklos* meaning "wheel")

Familiar Words with Root CYCL

- bicycle
- cyclist
- motorcycle
- tricycle

5. cycle (sī′ kəl)

n. A period of time during which events follow a certain pattern and repeat themselves.

The seasons change from one to another during a one-year cycle.

6. cyclone (sī′ klōn)

n. A strong whirling windstorm.

Thunderstorms surrounded the center of the tropical cyclone as it moved toward the coast.

Challenge Words with Root CYCL

- cyclic
- Cyclops
- cyclorama

7. recycle (rē sī′ kəl)

v. To treat or prepare in order to use again.

The factory recycled old newspapers to produce new paper products.

8. unicycle (yü′ ni sī kəl)
n. A vehicle with one wheel, usually moved by pedals.

It takes lots of practice to keep your balance while pedaling a unicycle.

EXERCISE A: SYNONYMS

Write the letter of the best SYNONYM (the word or phrase with the meaning most nearly the same as the word in bold-faced type).

1. ______ a dangerous **cyclone**

   a. accident b. event c. windstorm d. wheel

2. ______ a **circular** route

   a. curved b. level c. short d. difficult

3. ______ a two-year **cycle**

   a. job b. journey c. school d. time period

4. ______ an electrical **circuit**

   a. circus b. shock c. breaker d. route

5. ______ to **recycle** glass

   a. collect b. distribute c. fix for reuse d. wash

EXERCISE B: MEANING IN CONTEXT

Use these words to fill in the blanks in the following paragraph.

semicircle **unicycle** **circular** **cyclone** **circulate**

Members of our local One-Wheel Cyclists Club claim that anyone can learn to ride a (1) ____________________. The club members meet in a park that has both straight and (2) ____________________ paths for riding. Some of the more skilled members can pedal halfway around a circle and then pedal backwards over the same (3)____________________. At the meetings, newcomers often (4) ____________________ among the long-term members to hear about some interesting and unusual experiences. One rider likes to tell beginners about the time she was almost caught in a (5)____________________ and pedaled home as fast as she could while the wind and rain increased.

EXERCISE C: EXTEND YOUR VOCABULARY

The "one, two, three" prefixes: *uni-*, *bi-*, *tri-*

The numbers *one, two,* and *three* are connected with many words. In this lesson you met the word *unicycle,* and you learned that a unicycle has only one wheel. There are other words that start with *uni-*, and they also have a "one" connection. Look at the word ***unify,*** which means "to bring together as one."

In the box with Familiar Words, you see *bicycle* and *tricycle.* The prefix *bi-* has a "two" connection. A ***bi****cycle* has **two** wheels. A ***bi****ped* has **two** feet. The prefix *tri-* has a "three" connection. A ***tri****cycle* has **three** wheels. The dinosaur *triceratops* had **three** horns.

Underline the number prefix you see in each of these words. On the line beside the word, write the number and a short definition of the word.

1. triangle ______________________________

____

2. united ______________________________

____

3. bilingual ______________________________

____

4. unicorn ______________________________

____

5. triplets ______________________________

____

LESSON 2

Balancing Evenly

The root *equ* as in ***equivalent*** means "same, even, equal." The root *pend* as in *sus**pend**ers* means "hanging; weighing in the balance." In each of the following key words, underline the root.

Key Words

dependent	equate	equidistant	pending
equality	equator	equilateral	pendulum

Using ROOT CLUES

The roots *equ* (same) and *pend* (hanging) give you clues about meaning. When you spot one of these roots in a word, you have a key to the word's meaning. Use the underlined root clues to help you match the following columns:

1. ______	equidistant	A. hanging onto for support
2. ______	pendulum	B. same conditions or treatment
3. ______	equality	C. same distance
4. ______	dependent	D. hanging from a clock

The root clues did not give you complete definitions as the following dictionary listings will. But they got you started by giving you *part* of the meaning. Sometimes that *part* helps you to figure out the word.

EQU (from the Latin word *aequus* meaning "same, even, equal")

Familiar Words with Root EQU

- equal
- equally
- equivalent
- unequal

1. equality (i kwä′ lə tē)

n. The state of being equal, as in having the same value, measure, or rights.

The students argued that there had to be equality in the computer and science equipment available in all of the schools.

Challenge Words with Root EQU
equanimity
equilibrium
equinox
equitable

2. equate (i kwāt′)
v. To treat as the same or equivalent.

Both student papers are the same length, but we cannot equate them because so much more work and thought went into one of them.

equation, n.

3. equator (i kwā′ tər)
n. An imaginary line around the center of the earth, at the same distance from the North Pole and the South Pole.

The equator passes through many tropical countries, including Kenya in Africa and Brazil in South America.

4. equidistant (ē kwə dis′ tənt)
adj. Equally distant from two points.

Josh was pleased to learn that the ballpark was equidistant from both his home and his school, only two miles from each.

Familiar Words with Root PEND
depend
dependable
suspenders

5. equilateral (ē kwə la′ tə rəl) [also derived from the Latin *latus* meaning "side"]
adj. Having all sides equal in length.

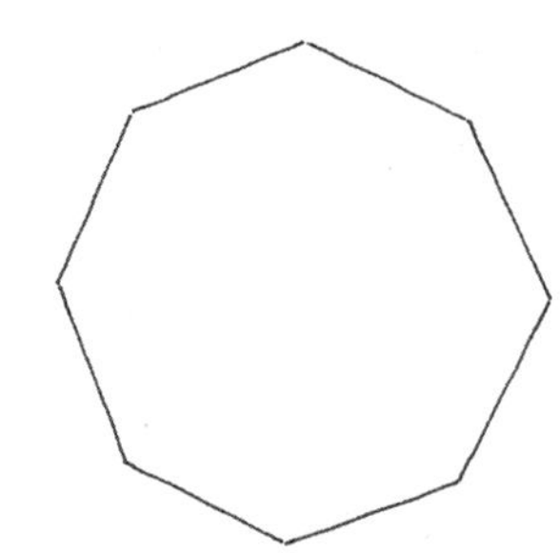

Each side of the octagon was the same length, so the figure was equilateral.

PEND (from the Latin word *pendo* meaning "hang")

Challenge Words with Root PEND
expendable
impending
pendant
pendulous
suspend
suspense

6. dependent (di pen′ dənt)
adj. Relying on another, looked after by someone else.

When Julia's baby brother cried and clung to her, she wished he was not so dependent.

7. pending (pen′ ding)
adj. Not yet decided; waiting to be concluded or finished.

The date for reopening the beach was pending, while the health department checked the bacteria level in the water.

8. pendulum (pen′ jə ləm)
n. A weight, hanging from a point, that swings an equal distance from side to side; often used in clocks.

The pendulum in the old clock, swinging in a regular arc, still kept accurate time.

EXERCISE A: SYNONYMS

Write the letter of the best SYNONYM (the word or phrase most nearly the same in meaning as the word in bold-faced type).

1. ______ an **equilateral** triangle
   a. equal sides b. right angles c. large d. yellow
2. ______ a **dependent** patient
   a. giving help b. needing help c. young d. angry
3. ______ working for **equality**
   a. liberty b. getting votes c. voting d. fairness
4. ______ the festival dates still **pending**
   a. undecided b. certain c. canceled d. posted
5. ______ to **equate** the situations
   a. describe b. make unfair c. treat as same d. criticize

EXERCISE B: MEANING IN CONTEXT

Use these words to fill in the blanks in the following paragraph.

equator **depending** **equidistant** **pendulum**

Rizzo's Clock Shop was easy to get to, right in the middle of the block, (1) ____________________ from each end. When I walked in, Mr. Rizzo was talking to a customer about a tall grandfather clock that had a long swinging (2) ____________________ and an unusual face. He said, "Many clocks have faces that are circular, like the (3) ____________________ that goes around our earth, but the face of this clock is shaped like an octagon. It is the only one of its kind, so I am (4) ____________________ on the person who buys it to treasure it."

EXERCISE C: EXTEND YOUR VOCABULARY

The "four" prefix: *quadr-*

One of the key words in this lesson is *equilateral,* which means "having sides that are equal." Looking at the two meaningful parts of this word, you recognize *equi,* "equal," and *lateral,* "side." In your math textbook, you may have met the word *quadrilateral.* Now let's use what you already know about *equilateral* to extend your vocabulary to *quadrilateral* and to other words that start with *quadr-.* Answer these questions.

1. Which figure is equilateral? ____________

A. **B.** **C.** **D.**

2. How many sides do you see on each of the preceding figures?

____

3. The preceding figures are called *quadrilaterals.* You know that one part of the word *quadrilateral* means "side." What does the other part mean?

____

4. The word *quadr*uplets refers to a certain number of babies. How many?

____

5. When you *quadr*uple an amount, by what number do you multiply?

____

LESSON 3

Moving Across and Between

The prefix *trans-* as in ***trans**portation* means "across." The prefix *inter-* as in ***inter**mediate* means "between." In each of the following key words, underline the prefix.

Key Words

interactive	intersect	transfer
interfere	interval	transfusion
intermittent	transact	transmit

Using PREFIX CLUES

The prefixes *trans-* (across) and *inter-* (between) give you clues about meaning. When you spot one of these prefixes in a word, you have a key to the word's meaning. Use the underlined prefix clues to help you match the following columns:

1. ______	interval	A. to send across
2. ______	transmit	B. with action between
3. ______	transfusion	C. a time between
4. ______	interactive	D. blood across (from one person to another)

The prefix clues did not give you complete definitions as the following dictionary listings will. But they got you started by giving you a *part* of the meaning. Sometimes that *part* helps you to figure out the word.

TRANS- (from Latin meaning "across")

Familiar Words with Prefix TRANS-

- transform
- transparent
- transplant
- transportation

1. transact (tran zakt′)
v. To do or carry on business.

On the Internet, people now can transact different kinds of business, from buying books to selling toys.

transaction, n.

Challenge Words with Prefix TRANS-

- transcribe
- transgress
- transitory
- translucent

2. transfer (tran(t)s fər′) [also derived from Latin *ferre* meaning "to carry"]

v. To move or change from one place to another.

On Saturday, we helped transfer the science equipment from the old lab on the first floor to the new one on the second.

n. A ticket for moving from one public vehicle to another to complete a trip. (tran(t)s′ fər)

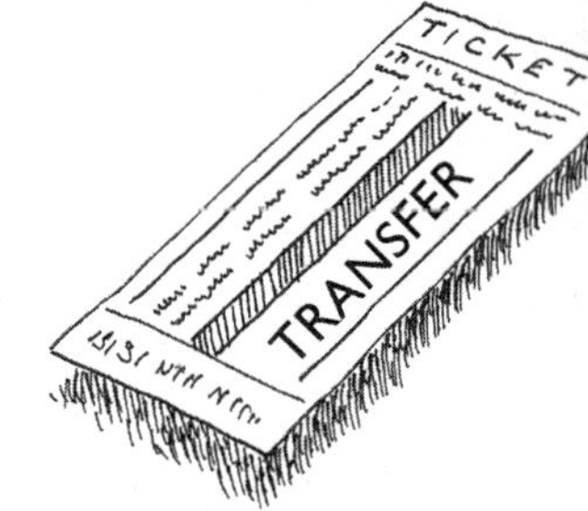

The bus driver gave Jessica a transfer so that she would not have to pay again on the connecting bus.

3. transfusion (tran(t)s fyü′ zhən) [also derived from the Latin *fundere* meaning "to pour"]

n. The movement of blood from one person to another by medical means.

During the operation, my aunt needed a transfusion.

4. transmit (tran(t)s mit′)

v. To send from one person or location to another.

Satellites allow television and radio stations to transmit their signals to distant locations.

INTER- (from Latin meaning "between")

Familiar Words with Prefix INTER-

- intermediate
- interstate

Challenge Words with Prefix INTER-

- interim
- interject
- interloper

5. interactive (in tər ak′ tiv)

adj. Able to act back and forth between people or things.

Laura likes to review vocabulary by completing interactive quizzes that she finds on the Internet.

6. interfere (in tər fir′) [also derived from Latin *ferire* meaning "to strike"]

v. 1. To come between.

At the theater, the head of a tall boy sitting in front of me interfered with my view of the screen.

2. To meddle or take part in other people's business without being invited.

Even though I didn't agree with how my sister was arranging the room, I didn't interfere.

7. intermittent (in tər mi′ tənt)

adj. Off-and-on, stop-and-start.

The dry fields needed steady rain but received only intermittent showers.

8. intersect (in tər sekt′)

v. To cut or pass through, to cross.

To get to the zoo, follow this street to where it intersects Carson Avenue, and then turn right.

intersection, n.

9. interval (in′ tər vəl)

n. Time or space between two events or objects.

Except for a two-day interval when he had a cold, Daniel went running every morning this month.

EXERCISE A: SYNONYMS

Write the letter of the best SYNONYM (the word or phrase with the meaning most nearly the same as the word in bold-faced type).

1. ______ lines that **intersect**

   a. cross　　b. curve　　c. parallel　　d. twist

2. ______ to **transfer** students

   a. teach　　b. grade　　c. move　　d. keep

3. ______ a blood **transfusion**

   a. spot　　b. loss　　c. clot　　d. transfer

4. ______ to **interfere** in

   a. perform　　b. sing　　c. meddle　　d. speak

5. ______ to **transact** business

   a. do　　b. lose　　c. look for　　d. miss

EXERCISE B: MEANING IN CONTEXT

Use these words to fill in the blanks in the following paragraph.

intermittent **transmit** **interactive** **interval**

Serena sat at the computer, working on an (1)____________ science program that responded each time she entered an answer. At the end of the program, she pressed SEND to (2)____________ her work to her teacher. She thought that after a short (3)____________ she would see her score on the monitor. But instead, her computer began making an (4)____________ beeping sound, a sure sign that she was not yet finished.

EXERCISE C: EXTEND YOUR VOCABULARY

The "cut" root: *sect*

You met the word *intersect* in this lesson. You know that *inter-* means "between." The "sect" part of *intersect* is derived from the Latin word *sectare,* meaning "to cut." Two streets that *intersect* "cut through" each other. The root *sect* also appears in the words *bisect, trisect,* and *section.*

Look at the words in the first column. Using your knowledge of word parts, find the correct meaning for each word in the second column. Then write its letter on the line before it.

1. ______ bisect A. to cut into three parts
2. ______ trisect B. a piece, cut from something
3. ______ section C. to cut into two parts
4. Choose one of the words and use it in a sentence.

____

____

Reviewing Lessons 1–3

EXERCISE A: MATCHING

Match each root or prefix with its meaning.

1. ______	circ	A. across
2. ______	cycl	B. between
3. ______	equ	C. hang
4. ______	pend	D. around
5. ______	trans-	E. revolving
6. ______	inter-	F. same

In Exercise C of Lessons 1, 2, and 3, you met these roots and prefixes. Match the columns.

7. ______	uni-	G. cut
8. ______	bi-	H. four
9. ______	tri-	I. two
10. ______	quadr-	J. one
11. ______	sect	K. three

Write sentences in which you use each of these words meaningfully.

12. quadrilateral ____

____

13. bisect ____

____

14. unify ____

____

EXERCISE B: SORTING

Sort these words, listing each one under its root or prefix. When you finish, add another word that goes with each group. (Look back at the lists of familiar and challenge words for ideas.)

circuit	**unicycle**	**intermittent**	**pending**
circular	**interfere**	**pendulum**	**semicircle**
dependent	**cyclone**	**equidistant**	**transact**
transmit	**equality**	**interval**	**equate**
intersect	**circulate**	**equator**	**interactive**
transfusion	**transfer**	**equilateral**	**cycle**
recycle			

1. CIRC

______
______
______
______
______
______

2. CYCL

______
______
______
______
______
______

3. EQU

______
______
______
______
______
______

4. PEND

______
______
______
______
______
______

5. TRANS-

______
______
______
______
______
______

6. INTER-

______
______
______
______
______
______

Write the answers to the following questions on the lines.

A. Which two columns contain words related to "going in circles"?

____

B. In which two columns do all the words have prefixes?

____

C. What are the meanings of the prefix and root in the word *unicycle*?

____

D. What are the meanings of the prefix and root in the word *intersect*?

____

EXERCISE C: VOCABULARY FROM YOUR TEXTBOOKS

Many of the subjects you are studying in school have specific words associated with them. Use these words to answer the following questions.

equilateral **circulate** **intersect** **circuit** **interactive**

1. As you read a lesson about blood vessels, which word might you see?

   ____

2. As you work on a lesson with crossing lines and equal-sided figures, what two words do you expect to see in the directions?

   ________________________________ ________________________________

3. When you make a poster to illustrate how electricity works, what word will you probably use?

   ____

4. When your teacher gives directions for using the new typing program on the computer, which word might he use as he describes it?

   ____

EXERCISE D: RHYMING RIDDLES

Write the letter of the answer for each riddle.

1. _____ What do you call a tropical reptile?
2. _____ What did the author say when she was not sure how to conclude her book?
3. _____ What do you call a leader of a school system who thinks for herself?
4. _____ What do you call a piece of jewelry that meddles?

A. Independent superintendent

B. Interfering earring

C. Equator alligator

D. Ending pending

EXERCISE E: WRITING AND DISCUSSION ACTIVITIES

1. Look at these headlines. Choose one. Then on the lines below, write a paragraph to tell what happened.

   A. Student Computer Whiz Develops Unusual Interactive Game

   B. Police Puzzled by Appearance of Ancient Pendulum at Headquarters

   C. Newspaper Recycling Leads to Surprising Problem

   ____

   ____

   ____

   ____

2. With a partner, compose a short conversation between <u>one</u> of these pairs of speakers. Make notes for your conversation on the lines below.

   A. A unicycle rider and a bicycle rider comparing the advantages of their vehicles

   B. A transfer student and a student in the school talking about what activities the school offers

   C. Two people at a flea market in the middle of transacting some business

   ____

   ____

3. Look back at the boxes of Challenge Words on pages 2, 6, and 10. From these words, choose three to write on the following lines. Try to define each word.

   A. ____________________

   B. ____________________

   C. ____________________

Now look up these three words in the dictionary. Expand (or revise) your definitions on the following lines.

   A. ____________________

   ____

   B. ____________________

   ____

   C. ____________________

   ____

LESSON 5

Looking at Our Planet

The root *aqua* as in ***aqua**rium* means "water." The root *terr* as in ***terr**arium* means "land." In each of the following key words, underline the root.

Key Words			
aquaculture	aquatic	subterranean	terrain
aquamarine	Mediterranean	terrace	territory

Using ROOT CLUES

The roots *aqua* (water) and *terr* (land) give you clues about meaning. When you spot one of these roots in a word, you have a key to the word's meaning. Use the underlined root clues to help you match the following columns:

1. ______	subterranean	A. color of sea water
2. ______	aquaculture	B. under the land
3. ______	territory	C. large area of land
4. ______	aquamarine	D. farming water creatures

The root clues did not give you complete definitions as the following dictionary listings will. But they got you started by giving you *part* of the meaning. Sometimes that *part* helps you figure out the word.

AQUA (from the Latin word *aqua* meaning "water")

Familiar Words with Root AQUA
aquarium
Aquarius

1. aquatic (ə kwä′ tik)

adj. Living in, or having to do with, water.

Whales, dolphins, shrimp, and guppies are all aquatic creatures.

Challenge Words with Root AQUA

- aqueduct
- aqueous
- aquifer

2. aquamarine (ä′ kwə mə rēn)

adj. A bluish-green color.

We watched as the artist mixed small amounts of both blue and green paints to make just the right shade of aquamarine for the seascape.

3. aquaculture (ä′ kwə kəl chər)

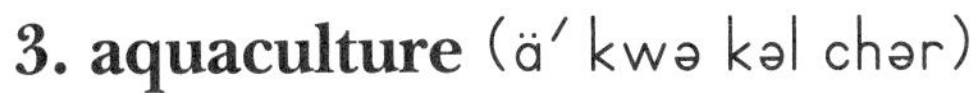

n. The science of raising plants and animals in water.

To see how aquaculture worked, we visited an oyster farm on the coast of Maine.

TERR (from the Latin word *terra* meaning "land")

Familiar Words with Root TERR

- extraterrestrial
- terrarium

Challenge Words with Root TERR

- terrazzo
- terrestrial

4. Mediterranean (me də tə rā′ nē ən)

n. A large sea between two continents, southern Europe and northern Africa.

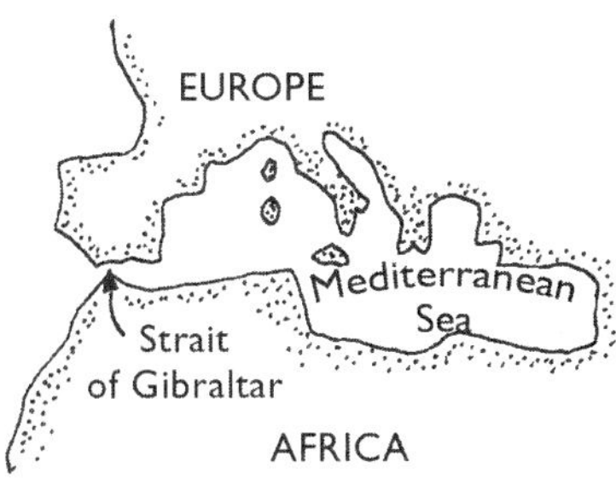

At the western end of the Mediterranean Sea is the Strait of Gibraltar.

NOTA BENE

The Mediterranean Sea was the center of civilization in the period of the Roman Empire when Latin was widely spoken. As you can see from the map above, this sea was truly in the middle (*medius*) of two huge lands (*terrae*).

5. subterranean (səb tə rā′ nē ən)

adj. Under the earth.

New York City's subway trains travel through hundreds of miles of subterranean passages.

6. terrace (ter′ əs)

n. 1. An area of ground on the side of a hill that has a flattened top in order to grow things.

We could see terraces all the way up the hillside where farmers had planted their crops.

2. A platform built out from a house; a patio.

In good weather, our family often eats outside on the terrace.

7. terrain (tə rān′)

n. Land or ground.

The truck bumped along on the rough terrain of the field until it reached a paved road on the other side.

8. territory (ter′ ə tōr ē)

n. A large area of land, a region; a settlement or colony.

In 1803 the United States purchased the Louisiana Territory, which added about eight hundred thousand square miles of land to the country.

EXERCISE A: SYNONYMS

Write the letter of the best SYNONYM (the word or phrase most nearly the same in meaning as the word in bold-faced type).

1. ______ **subterranean** oil

   a. expensive b. thick c. underground d. dark

2. ______ an **aquaculture** business

   a. diving b. flying c. hiking d. farming in water

3. ______ a wooden **terrace**

   a. fountain b. outdoor platform c. house d. sign

4. ______ **aquatic** plants

   a. in the air b. on land c. in water d. in caves

5. ______ a large **territory**

   a. region b. ocean c. continent d. river

EXERCISE B: MEANING IN CONTEXT

Use these words to fill in the blanks in the following paragraph.

aquatic **terrain** **aquamarine** **Mediterranean**

The lands around the (1)______________ Sea have a variety of features. Some have soil that is good for farming, while others have rocky hills and rough

(2)____________________ where planting anything would be difficult. From some points on the seacoast, the water looks clear; in other places it appears to be a deep shade of (3)____________________. In shallow spots, you can see (4)____________________ plants growing underwater.

EXERCISE C: EXTEND YOUR VOCABULARY

The "sea" root: *marin*

One of the key words in this lesson is *aquamarine.* It has two meaningful parts, *aqua* and *marine. Marine* is derived from the Latin word *marinus,* meaning "belonging to the sea" or "of the sea." So the meaning of *aquamarine* can be pieced together as "water of the sea." Seawater sometimes seems to have a blue-green color, which explains the definition of *aquamarine.*

The root *marin* also appears in other words connected with the sea.

Match the words with the root *marin* with their meaning.

1. ______ person guiding a ship — A. marina
2. ______ underwater ship — B. marine plant
3. ______ place for docking boats — C. submarine
4. ______ seaweed — D. mariner
5. Use two of the words with the root *marin* in sentences of your own.

____

____

____

____

Exploring Distant Places

The root *tele* as in ***tele**vision* means "far away." The root *astr* as in ***astr**onomer* means "star; outer space." In each of the following key words, underline the root.

Key Words

astronaut	astronomy	teleconference	telemarketing
astronomical	telecast	telegraph	telescope

Using ROOT CLUES

The roots *tele* (far) and *astr* (outer space) give you clues about meaning. When you spot one of these roots in a word, you have a key to the word's meaning. Use the underlined root clues to help you match the following columns:

1. ______ <u>tele</u>scope — A. selling from a<u>far</u>, not face-to-face
2. ______ <u>astr</u>onaut — B. science of <u>outer space</u>
3. ______ <u>tele</u>marketing — C. traveler in <u>outer space</u>
4. ______ <u>astr</u>onomy — D. device for seeing <u>far</u>-away objects

The root clues did not give you complete definitions as the following dictionary listings will. But they got you started by giving you *part* of the meaning. Sometimes that *part* helps you to figure out the word.

TELE (from the Greek word *tele* meaning "distant; far away")

Familiar Words with Root TELE

telephone
television

1. telecast (te′ li kast)

n. A broadcast by television.

In 1969, a telecast of the first landing of human beings on the moon was viewed around the world.

Challenge Words with Root TELE
telecommunication
telepathy
telethon

2. teleconference (te′ li kän′ fə rə(t)s)
n. A meeting at which people see and talk to each other using long-distance devices, such as telephones, televisions, and computers.

During the teleconference, students in our school could talk with students in London.

3. telegraph (te′ lə graf)
n. An instrument invented in 1837 by Samuel Morse that used electricity passing through wires to send messages over distances.

By the 1860s, the telegraph had become the fastest way to send a message from one city to another.

4. telemarketing (te lə mär′ kə ting)
n. Selling by telephone.

While telemarketing has been popular with businesses, the people receiving the phone calls are not always so pleased.

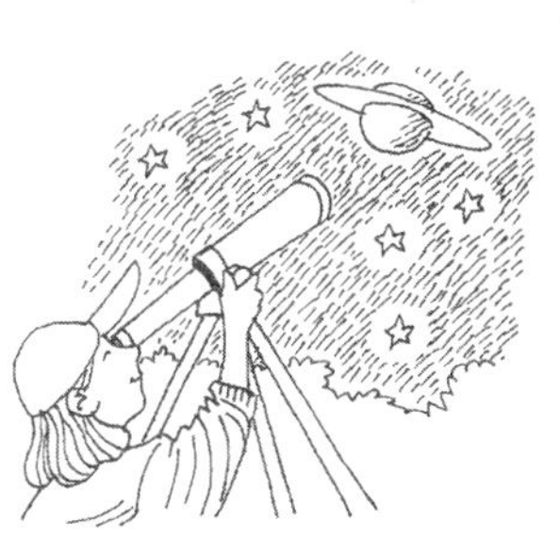

5. telescope (te′ lə skōp)
n. An instrument for making distant objects look closer and larger.

Through her telescope, Olivia could see the rings around Saturn.

ASTR (from the Greek word *aster* and the Latin word *astrum* meaning "star; outer space")

Familiar Words with Root ASTR
astronomer
disaster

6. astronaut (as′ trə not) [also derived from the Greek *nautilos* meaning "sailor or traveler"]
n. Space traveler.

In 1983, Sally Ride became the first female astronaut to complete a mission to outer space.

7. astronomical (as′ trə nä′ mi kəl)
adj. 1. Extremely large, huge.

The distance among the stars in the Milky Way is astronomical.

Challenge Words with Root ASTR

- asterisk
- asteroid
- astral
- astrodome
- astrolabe

2. Related to astronomy.

Light-year, the measurement of the distance light travels in a year, is a term used often in astronomical discussions.

8. astronomy (ə strä′ nə mē)

n. The branch of science for the study of planets, stars, and space.

After her course in astronomy, Tameka could point out the stars in the constellation Aquarius.

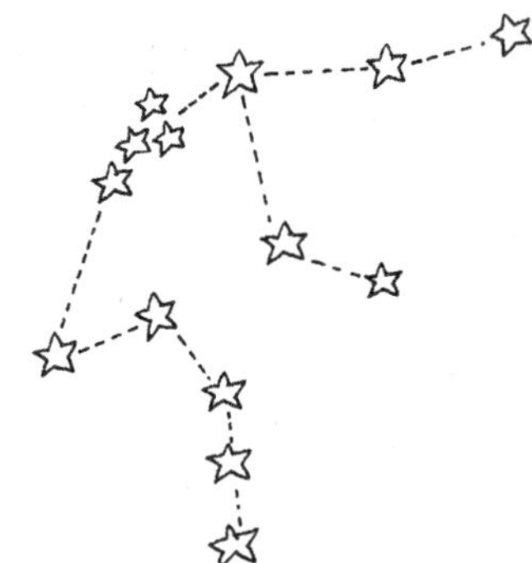

NOTA BENE

In your social studies textbook, you may have met another word with the *astr* root: *astrolabe.* Long ago, sailors used an astrolabe to determine their location at sea by measuring the altitude of the stars.

EXERCISE A: SYNONYMS

Write the letter of the best SYNONYM (the word or phrase most nearly the same in meaning as the word in bold-faced type).

1. ______ learning about **astronomy**

   a. space travel b. science of space c. space scientist d. starship

2. ______ a long **teleconference**

   a. meeting b. series c. announcement d. view

3. ______ an **astronomical** figure

   a. distant b. important c. medium d. huge

4. ______ to send by **telegraph**

   a. horse b. train c. electrical currents through wires d. fax machine

5. ______ the job of **telemarketing**

   a. writing b. editing c. mailing d. phoning

EXERCISE B: MEANING IN CONTEXT

Use these words to fill in the blanks in the following paragraph.

astronaut **telecast** **astronomy** **teleconference** **telescope**

Miguel turned on the television to watch the (1)________________ he had been waiting a week to see. Tonight two of his heroes were going to be interviewed for an hour. They were an engineer who had worked on moon landings and an (2)________________ who had traveled to the moon. Miguel had a (3)________________ in his backyard, and he often looked at the moon's changes. He hoped that someday he could walk on its surface. Last year, his science teacher had set up a (4)________________ so that he and other members of the (5)________________ club could ask questions of scientists at the local university. But tonight, Miguel would be able to hear someone who had actually been on the moon.

EXERCISE C: EXTEND YOUR VOCABULARY

The "instrument" root: *scope*

The word *telescope* has two meaningful parts: *tele* and *scope*. You know that *tele* means "far away." *Scope* is derived from the Greek word *skopein* meaning "to see." A *telescope* helps you *see* objects in space that are *far away*.

Here are some more instruments that include *scope*. Match each of them with what it helps you see.

1. _____ microscope A. changing patterns in a tube that you can twist
2. _____ periscope B. very tiny items
3. _____ kaleidoscope C. the inside of the eye
4. _____ ophthalmoscope D. things that are above, as from a submarine

Below each of the following pictures, write the name of the correct "scope."

1.

____

2.

____

3.

____

4.

____

LESSON 7

Changing Meaning with Prefixes

The prefix *in-* can mean "not" as in ***in**correct*. The prefix *semi-* can mean "half" or "partly," as in ***semi**private*. In each of the following key words, underline the prefix.

Key Words

inactive	insomnia	semiconscious
informal	semiannual	semiformal
insignificant	semicolon	semiprecious

Using PREFIX CLUES

The prefixes *in-* (not) and *semi-* (half) give you clues about meaning. When you spot one of these prefixes in a word, you have a key to the word's meaning. Use the underlined prefix clues to match the following columns:

1. ______	<u>semi</u>conscious	A. <u>not</u> exercising
2. ______	<u>in</u>active	B. <u>not</u> important
3. ______	<u>semi</u>annual	C. <u>half</u> a year
4. ______	<u>in</u>significant	D. <u>half</u> awake

The prefix clues did not give you complete definitions as the following dictionary listings will. But they got you started by giving you *part* of the meaning. Sometimes that *part* helps you to figure out the word.

IN- (from Latin meaning "not")

Familiar Words with Prefix IN-

- incomplete
- inconvenient
- incorrect
- infrequent

Challenge Words with Prefix IN-

- inadequate
- incapable
- incomparable
- indecisive
- indefinite
- insincere

1. inactive (i nak′ tiv)

adj. 1. Not moving or active.

The summer heat kept even our energetic puppy inactive.

2. No longer in use.

When summer ends, the small ferry that carries people across the lake becomes inactive.

2. informal (in for′ məl)

adj. Casual, relaxed, not formal.

After her speech, the author attended an informal reception in the library where she answered questions.

3. insignificant (in(t) sig ni′ fi kənt) [also derived from Latin *significare* meaning "to signify"]

adj. Not significant, unimportant, lacking power or value.

An insignificant amount of snow fell last night, leaving only a dusting on the streets.

4. insomnia (in säm′ nē ə)[also derived from Latin *somnus* meaning "sleep"]

n. An ongoing condition of being unable to fall or stay asleep.

Because of her insomnia, Sarah's mother kept a book by the bed so she could read when she awoke in the middle of the night.

NOTA BENE

In is a complete word by itself as well as a meaningful part of other words. Example: The gift is in the box. In that example, the word *in* means "within." Sometimes *in* carries the same "within" meaning as a prefix—on words like *inside, inland,* and *internal.* The prefix *in-*, like many other prefixes, has more than one meaning. The words featured in this lesson demonstrate the "not" meaning of the prefix *in-*.

SEMI- (from Latin meaning "half or partly")

Familiar Words with Prefix SEMI-
semifinal
semiprivate
semisweet

Challenge Words with Prefix SEMI-
semidetached
semiprofessional

5. semiannual (se mē an′ yə wəl)
[also derived from Latin *annus* meaning "year"]
adj. Occurring in half a year, every six months.

Our semiannual neighborhood cleanups take place in April and October.

6. semicolon (se′ mē kō lən)
n. A punctuation mark that signals a break in a sentence, halfway between the full stop of a period and the short pause of a comma.

A semicolon looks like a dot over a comma; it separates two independent clauses in a sentence.

7. semiconscious (se mē kän(t)′ shəs)
adj. Half or partly awake, not fully conscious, in a daze.

After the removal of his tonsils, Eric was in a semiconscious state in the recovery room.

8. semiformal (se mē for′ məl)
adj. Requiring good clothes rather than play clothes.

Natalie attended the wedding in a semiformal outfit, but the bridesmaids wore formal gowns.

9. semiprecious (se mē pre′ shəs)
adj. Having only part of the value of a precious gemstone.

Semiprecious stones like opals have value but not as much as precious stones like diamonds, emeralds, and rubies.

 EXERCISE A: SYNONYMS

Write the letter of the best SYNONYM (word or phrase that is closest in meaning to the word in bold-faced type).

1. ______ using a **semicolon**

a. number b. punctuation mark c. letter d. abbreviation

2. ______ a **semiprecious** stone

a. having the highest value
b. having partial value
c. having no value
d. brand new

3. ______ their **semiformal** outfits

a. dirty b. patched c. blue d. dressy

4. ______ **insignificant** gossip

a. whispered b. unimportant c. colorful d. loud

5. ______ a **semiconscious** state

a. dazed b. alert c. unhappy d. sick

EXERCISE B: MEANING IN CONTEXT

Use these words to fill in the blanks in the following paragraph.

semiannual **insomnia** **insignificant** **inactive**

Brenda knew it made no sense to fret over something as (1)______________ as losing a game of chess. But in the middle of the night she was still wide awake with (2)______________. How had her cousin Sam beaten her so easily? Sam and his parents were visiting her family as they usually did every six months. On these (3)______________ visits she and Sam always played chess, and Brenda usually won. But this time it had been different. Then she remembered. Sam had injured himself in a soccer game and was on the team's (4)______________ list. He probably had played a lot of chess instead. Brenda decided that losing a chess game to Sam was completely understandable, and she quickly fell asleep.

EXERCISE C: EXTEND YOUR VOCABULARY

Other spellings of the prefix *in-*: *ig-*, *il-*, *im-*, *ir-*

The prefix *in-* has several spelling variations, but they all mean "not." ***Ignore*** means **not** to notice. ***Illegal*** means **not** legal. ***Impossible*** means **not** possible. ***Irresistible*** means **not** able to be resisted.

Sort the following twelve words, listing them by the spelling of the prefix.

impatient	**illiterate**	**imperfect**	**irremovable**
irregular	**irreplaceable**	**ignoble**	**irresponsible**
immovable	**illogical**	**impractical**	**immature**

IG-

____
____
____
____
____

IL-

____
____
____
____
____

IM-

____
____
____
____
____

IR-

____
____
____
____
____

Reread the twelve words you sorted.

1. How many started with *ig-*? ______________
2. How many started with *il-*? ______________
3. How many started with *im-*? ______________
4. How many started with *ir-*? ______________
5. What is the meaning of all four of these prefixes? ______________

Other negative prefixes

There are other prefixes that also mean "not."

6. What does *un-* mean in the word *unlucky*? ____________________
7. What does *dis-* mean in *disagree*? ____________________
8. What does *non-* mean in *nonfiction*? ____________________
9. Write another word that starts with each of the prefixes *un-*, *dis-*, and *non-*.

____

____

____

10. Use each of the words you wrote in a sentence.

____

____

____

____

____

____

LESSON 8

Reviewing Lessons 5–7

EXERCISE A: MATCHING

Match each root or prefix with its meaning.

1. ______	aqua	A. space
2. ______	terr	B. land
3. ______	astr	C. partly or half
4. ______	tele	D. not
5. ______	in-	E. far or distant
6. ______	semi-	F. water

In Exercise C of Lessons 5, 6, and 7, you met these roots and prefixes. Match the columns. (You will use one of the letters twice.)

7. ______	marin	G. not
8. ______	ig-, il-, im-, ir-	H. instrument
9. ______	scope	I. sea
10. ______	non-, un-, dis-	

EXERCISE B: SORTING

Sort these words, listing each one under its root or prefix. When you finish, add another word that goes with each group. (Look back at the lists of familiar and challenge words for ideas.)

telecast	**aquaculture**	**astronaut**	**informal**
semicolon	**telescope**	**territory**	**Mediterranean**
astronomy	**semiformal**	**insignificant**	**semiconscious**
insomnia	**astronomical**	**telegraph**	**teleconference**
subterranean	**aquamarine**	**inactive**	**terrain**
aquatic	**terrace**	**telemarketing**	**semiannual**
semiprecious			

1. AQUA

____
____
____
____
____
____

2. TERR

____
____
____
____
____
____

3. ASTR

____
____
____
____
____
____

4. TELE

____
____
____
____
____
____

5. IN-

____
____
____
____
____
____

6. SEMI-

____
____
____
____
____
____

In the blanks, write the answers for the following questions.

A. In which two columns do you find words related to seeing or hearing at a distance?

____

B. In which column do you find a word for a punctuation mark?

____

C. What are the meanings of the two parts of the word *telescope*?

____

D. What are the meanings of the two parts of the word *aquamarine*?

____

EXERCISE C: VOCABULARY FROM YOUR TEXTBOOKS

Many of the subjects you are studying in school have specific words associated with them. Use these words to answer the following questions.

telegraph **semiprecious** **telescope** **semicolon** **astronomical**

1. If you were reading a lesson on punctuation, which word would you see?

   ____

2. In a chapter about the solar system, which two words would you probably meet?

   ______________________________ ______________________________

3. While you are doing a Web search for a report on gems and other valuable stones, which word are you likely to see?

   ____

4. When you read about the life of Samuel Morse for a book report, which word will you find?

   ____

EXERCISE D: RHYMING RIDDLES

Write the letter of the answer for each rhyming riddle.

1. _____ What do you call a person aged thirteen to nineteen with blue-green skin?
2. _____ What do you call the final news report on TV?
3. _____ What do you call land with little to see?
4. _____ What do you call a guidebook that is issued twice a year?
5. _____ What do you call a tale about a big region of land?

A. Last telecast

B. Aquamarine teen

C. Plain terrain

D. Territory story

E. Semiannual manual

EXERCISE E: WRITING AND DISCUSSION ACTIVITIES

1. Look at these headlines. Choose one. Then on the lines below, write a paragraph to tell what happened.

   A. Teleconference Ends Suddenly Leaving Participants Puzzled

   B. Aquaculture Farmer Displays New Fish

   C. Students Change to Semiformal Clothes for School

   ____

   ____

   ____

   ____

2. With a partner, compose a short conversation between one of these pairs of speakers. Make notes for your conversation on the lines below.

   A. An astronaut circling the earth and a student on a Mediterranean cruise discussing what they are seeing on their travels

   B. A person returning from an aquatic vacation and someone whose vacation was spent exploring subterranean caves comparing their adventures

   C. A person with insomnia asking a doctor for advice on how to get a good night's sleep

   ____

   ____

3. Look back at the boxes of Challenge Words on pages 19, 23, 24, 27, and 28. From these words, choose three to write on the following lines. Try to define each word.

   A. ____

   B. ____

   C. ____

Now look up these three words in the dictionary. Expand (or revise) your definitions on the following lines.

   A. ____

   B. ____

   C. ____

Creating Order

The root *civi* as in ***civilize*** means "relating to citizens." The root *ord* as in ***order*** means "regular." In each of the following key words, underline the root.

Key Words

civics	civilian	coordinate	ordinarily
civil	civility	extraordinary	uncivilized

Using ROOT CLUES

The roots *civi* (citizen) and *ord* (regular) give you clues about meaning. When you spot one of these roots in a word, you have a key to the word's meaning. Use the underlined root clues to help you match the following columns:

1. _____	<u>ord</u>inarily	A. more than <u>regular</u>
2. _____	un<u>civi</u>lized	B. in the <u>regular</u> way
3. _____	extra<u>ord</u>inary	C. related to life as a <u>citizen</u>
4. _____	<u>civi</u>l	D. not having the organized life of a <u>citizen</u>

The root clues did not give you complete definitions as the following dictionary listings will. But they got you started by giving you *part* of the meaning. Sometimes that *part* helps you to figure out the word. In addition, the prefix clues were helpful—*un-* meaning "not," and *extra-* meaning "more than."

CIVI (from the Latin word *civis* meaning "citizen, a member of a city")

Familiar Words with Root CIVI

civilization

civilize

1. civics (si′ viks)

n. The study of a citizen's rights and duties in a society.

In the course on civics, Juan learned how the three branches of the United Sates government worked.

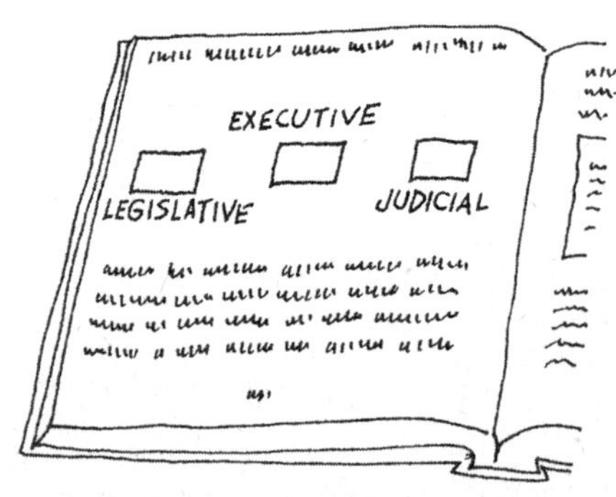

Challenge Words with Root CIVI

- civil disobedience
- civil engineer
- civil rights
- civil war

2. civil (si′ vəl)

adj. 1. Having to do with citizens and their relation to each other and to the government.

My parents always vote because they believe it is the most important civil duty.

2. Fairly courteous.

Although Jasmine was angry with her friend, she managed to give a civil answer to his question.

3. civilian (sə vil′ yən)

n. A person who is not in the military.

Many countries agree that during war civilians should not be attacked by those who are fighting.

adj. Relating to civil life, not military.

After serving in the navy for two years, my brother returned to civilian life.

4. civility (sə vi′ li tē)

n. Courteous behavior.

Nathan greeted his unwelcome visitors with civility, but not with affection.

5. uncivilized (ən si′ və līzd)

adj. 1. Without an organized or developed society, wild.

The Chinese believed that the Mongols, who took over their kingdom in the thirteenth century, were uncivilized.

2. Acting without courtesy or consideration.

"Don't be so uncivilized!" exclaimed my aunt, as I chatted away with food in my mouth.

ORD (from the Latin word *ordo* meaning "regularity, order")

Familiar Words with Root ORD

disorder
order
orderly
orderliness
reorder

Challenge Words with Root ORD

inordinate
insubordination
ordinal
ordinance

6. coordinate (kō or′ də nāt)
v. To bring together to work smoothly.

Kevin and Brianna coordinated the registration for summer swimming classes.

7. extraordinary (ik stror′ dən er ē)
adj. More than the ordinary, beyond what is expected, remarkable.

The extraordinary length of the Mississippi River makes it one of the ten longest rivers in the world.

8. ordinarily (or dən er′ ə lē)
adv. Usually, generally, in the regular way.

Ordinarily, I take my piano lesson at one o'clock on Saturdays, but next week I'll take it at two.

EXERCISE A: ANTONYMS

Write the letter of the best ANTONYM (the word or phrase most nearly opposite in meaning to the word in bold-faced type).

1. ______ a group of **civilians**
   a. doctors   b. soldiers   c. governors   d. teachers
2. ______ an **extraordinary** storm
   a. fine   b. better   c. common   d. terrifying
3. ______ **uncivilized** behavior
   a. rich   b. healthy   c. uneducated   d. courteous
4. ______ was dressed **ordinarily**
   a. unusually   b. fairly   c. quickly   d. neatly
5. ______ acted with **civility**
   a. order   b. enthusiasm   c. rudeness   d. kindness

EXERCISE B: MEANING IN CONTEXT

Use these words to fill in the blanks in the following paragraph.

civics **extraordinary** **coordinated** **civil**

Ms. Weber teaches classes in two related subjects, United States history and (1)____________________, the study of our government. In both classes, she teaches about Martin Luther King Jr., who (2)____________________ the drive for legislation that would ensure equality for everyone. Her students say that after studying with her, they have a much better understanding of Dr. King's role in the (3)____________________ rights movement. They can see clearly what an (4)____________________ time it was.

EXERCISE C: EXTEND YOUR VOCABULARY

The noun suffix *-ity*

One of the key words in this lesson is *civility*. It ends with the suffix *-ity*. This suffix shows that a word is a noun. The meaning of a noun ending in *-ity* is usually connected to the meaning of its adjective partner. *Civility* is related to "being *civil*," just as *equality* is related to "being *equal*." *Civil* and *equal* are adjectives. *Civil**ity*** and *equal**ity*** are nouns.

All of the nouns in the first column end in the suffix *-ity*. On the line, write the adjective from which the noun was formed.

Nouns	**Adjectives**
1. activity	____________________
2. possibility	____________________
3. vitality	____________________
4. originality	____________________
5. creativity	____________________

6. Choose two of the nouns and use each one in a sentence.

____

____

____

____

LESSON 10

Measuring in Math and Science

The root *metr/meter* as in ***metric*** means "measurement." The root *therm* as in ***thermos*** means "heat." In each of the following key words, underline the root.

Key Words

diameter	metronome	symmetrical	thermometer
geometry	perimeter	thermal	thermostat

Using ROOT CLUES

The roots *metr/meter* (measurement) and *therm* (heat) give you clues about meaning. When you spot one of these roots in a word, you have a key to the word's meaning. Use the underlined root clues to help you match the following columns:

1. _____	thermal	A. measurement of outside boundary
2. _____	perimeter	B. having to do with heat
3. _____	thermostat	C. the study of the measurement of shapes
4. _____	geometry	D. device for controlling heat

The root clues did not give you complete definitions as the following dictionary listings will. But they got you started by giving you *part* of the meaning. Sometimes that *part* helps you to figure out the word.

METR/METER (from the Greek word *metron* meaning "measure")

Familiar Words with Root METR/METER

meter
metric

1. diameter (dī a′ mə tər) [also derived from Greek *dia* meaning "through"]

n. A line passing through the center of a circle from one side to the other.

Kylie created two semicircles by drawing the diameter through the circle.

Challenge Words with Root METR/METER

- chronometer
- trigonometry
- biometric

2. **geometry** (jē ä′ mə trē) [also derived from Greek *ge* meaning "earth"]
   n. The area of mathematics that deals with lines, angles, and figures and their measurements.

   When studying geometry, we will learn how to measure the size of different kinds of figures.

   geometric, adj.

3. **metronome** (me′ trə nōm)
   n. A device that marks the beat for musicians.

   Mr. Rogers, our band leader, set the metronome to tick the quick tempo of a march.

4. **perimeter** (pə ri′ mə tər) [also derived from Greek *peri* meaning "around"]
   n. The distance around a figure.

   Before ordering the materials for a fence to enclose her yard, Aunt Anna measured its perimeter.

5. **symmetrical** (sə me′ tri kəl) [also derived from Greek *syn* meaning "together"]
   adj. Similar in shape and size on opposite sides of a dividing line.

   Carlos folded the paper in half so that as he cut out the bird shape the sides would be symmetrical.

NOTA BENE

Meter is a complete word in itself as well as a meaningful part of other words. It means the basic unit of length in the metric system, a measurement of 39.37 inches, which is a little longer than a yard.

THERM (from the Greek word *therme* meaning "heat")

Familiar Words with Root THERM

- thermos

6. **thermal** (thər′ məl)
   adj. Warm, hot, having to do with heat.

   The temperature of the water in the thermal spring was higher than the temperature of the air around it.

Challenge Words with Root THERM
thermodynamics
thermoelectric
thermoplastic

7. thermometer (thər′ mä mə tər)

n. An instrument for measuring the temperature of a person or place.

The nurse put a thermometer in my mouth to see if I had a fever.

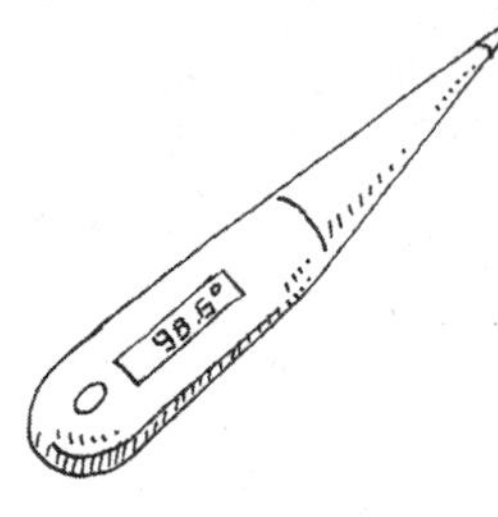

8. thermostat (thər′ mə stat)

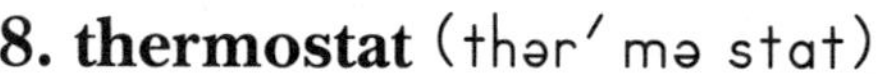

n. A device for regulating heat.

Before going to bed, Dad set the thermostat to turn on the heat if the temperature dropped during the night.

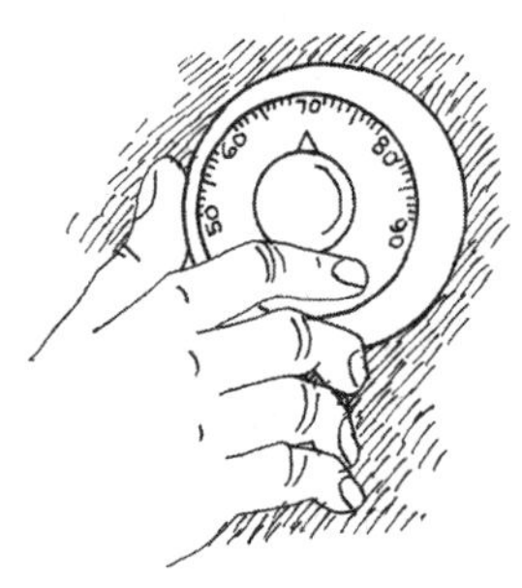

EXERCISE A: SYNONYMS

Write the letter of the best SYNONYM (the word or phrase most nearly the same in meaning as the word in bold-faced type).

1. ______ measure the **diameter**

   a. curve b. circle c. line d. arc

2. ______ a **thermal** system

   a. difficult b. heating c. grading d. drawing

3. ______ adjusted the **thermostat**

   a. sound b. light c. temperature d. speed

4. ______ **symmetrical** parts

   a. intersecting b. warm c. cold d. similar

5. ______ using a **metronome**

   a. timekeeper b. metal bar c. musical instrument d. subway

EXERCISE B: MEANING IN CONTEXT

Use these words to fill in the blanks in the following paragraph.

perimeter **thermometer** **geometry** **thermal**

When working outdoors in Alaska, the surveyors from Louisiana wore (1)________________ underwear to preserve their body heat, but they were still cold. The morning that the (2)________________ showed a temperature below zero, they put on extra layers of clothing, but they were still cold. These surveyors were smart. They had studied (3)_________________ and knew how to correctly mark the boundaries of large pieces of land. They had no difficulty measuring the (4)_________________ of what they had marked. What they didn't know was how to get used to the cold.

EXERCISE C: EXTEND YOUR VOCABULARY

The "thousand" prefixes: *kilo-* and *milli-*

Kilo and *milli* (which appear with *meter*) are meaningful word parts. In the metric measuring system *kilo-* (from Greek for thousand) means "one thousand" and *milli-* (from Latin for thousand) means "one part of one thousand." A kilometer is 1000 meters. A millimeter is 1/1000 of a meter.

Using what you know from these meaningful parts, answer the following questions:

1. Is a *kilogram* lighter or heavier than a gram?

   ____

2. Is a *milligram* lighter or heavier than a gram?

   ____

3. Do you think a *milliliter* has more or less liquid than a liter?

   ____

4. Do you think a *kiloliter* has more or less liquid than a liter?

   ____

Among the key words in this lesson are *perimeter, diameter*, and *thermometer*. *Meter* is a meaningful part of many other words too. Match each "meter" word in Column 1 with what it could measure in Column 2.

5. ______	speedometer	A. distance between cities
6. ______	kilometer	B. a line less than a centimeter long
7. ______	millimeter	C. atmospheric pressure for predicting the weather
8. ______	barometer	D. miles per hour in a car

LESSON 11

Pulling Together

The root *struct* as in ***struct**ure* means "build." The root *tract* as in ***tract**or* means "pull, drag." In each of the following key words, underline the root.

Key Words

construction	extract	retract
contraction	protractor	structure
destructive	reconstruct	traction

Using ROOT CLUES

The roots *struct* (build) and *tract* (pull) give you clues about meaning. When you spot one of these roots in a word, you have a key to the word's meaning. Use the underlined root clues to help you match the following columns:

1. ______	con<u>tract</u>ion	A. to <u>build</u> again
2. ______	recon<u>struct</u>	B. to <u>pull</u> back
3. ______	<u>struct</u>ure	C. a <u>pull</u>ing together
4. ______	re<u>tract</u>	D. a <u>build</u>ing

The root clues did not give you complete definitions as the following dictionary listings will. But they got you started by giving you *part* of the meaning. Sometimes that *part* helps you to figure out the word.

STRUCT (from the Latin word *struere* meaning "to heap up, build")

Familiar Words with Root STRUCT
- construct
- instruct
- instructions

1. construction (kən strək′ shən)
n. The act of putting something together in an organized way; building.

Jocelyn laid out all the parts before starting the construction of her model airplane.

Challenge Words with Root STRUCT
obstruct
restructure
structurally
superstructure

2. destructive (di strək′ tiv)

adj. Tearing down; likely to discourage, ruin, destroy, put an end to.

The storm's destructive winds brought down many tree branches.

3. reconstruct (rē kən strəkt′)

v. To build again, to make over.

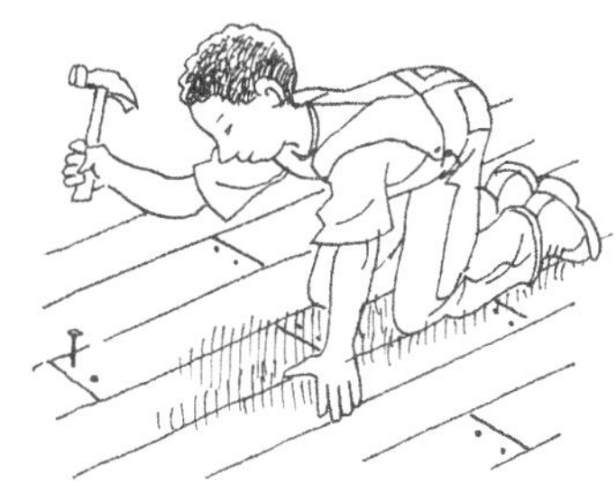

When they reconstructed the old house, the builders used many of the original floorboards.

4. structure (strək′ chər)

n. 1. The arrangement of the parts of a whole.

When studying sentence structure, you learn that word order is important.

2. Something built, constructed, organized.

Adobe mud-brick structures often have cool interiors.

TRACT (from the Latin word *tractus* meaning "to pull")

Familiar Words with Root TRACT
attract
subtract
subtraction
tractor

Challenge Words with Root TRACT
detract
distraction
intractable

5. contraction (kən trak′ shən)

n. 1. A shortening of two words, such as *isn't* for "is not."

The contraction *they'd* can mean "they had" or "they would."

2. The thickening and hardening of a muscle in action.

Swimming across the small lake, Jayden felt a sudden contraction in his foot, cramping his toes.

6. extract (ik strakt′)

v. 1. To pull out or remove by force.

The dentist said she would need to extract the tooth.

2. To draw out by processing.

The chemist dissolved the iron ore in acid to extract the iron.

n. A concentrated form of a substance. (ek′ strakt)

It took only a little vanilla extract to add a lot of vanilla flavor to the cake.

7. protractor (prō trak′ tər)

n. A semicircular device for drawing and measuring angles.

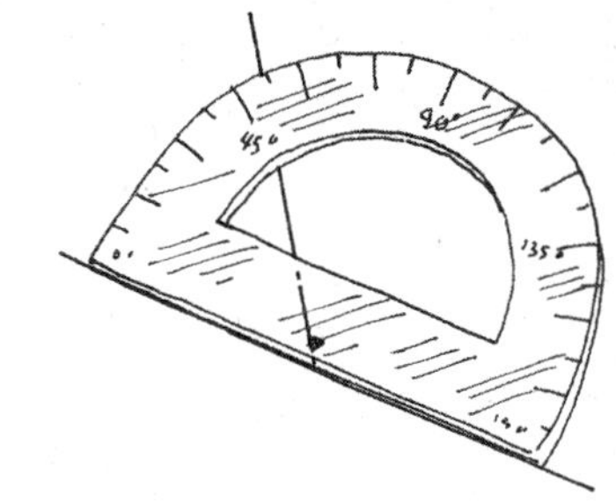

When Dominic placed his protractor on top of the angle, he could see the number of degrees it had.

8. retract (ri trakt′)

v. 1. To take back or withdraw.

When the teacher wasn't amused, Kaitlyn retracted her statement that the dog had eaten her homework.

2. To draw back or in.

The sunroof of the car retracted and fresh air filled the car.

9. traction (trak′ shən)

n. 1. The power to grip or hold to a surface.

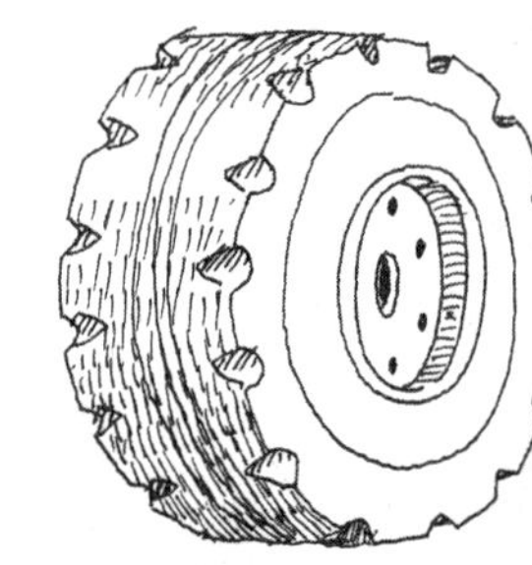

Our new tires had good traction, which kept our car from sliding on the ice.

2. A pulling on part of the body to help in healing.

At the hospital, my leg was put in traction for several days.

EXERCISE A: ANTONYMS

Write the letter of the best ANTONYM (the word or phrase most nearly opposite in meaning to the word in bold-faced type).

1. ______ to **extract** the tooth

a. pull b. fill c. drill d. implant

2. ______ rapid **construction**

a. carpenters b. destruction c. bricks d. building

3. ______ **retract** a claim

a. review b. take back c. persist in d. speak

4. ______ **destructive** words

a. angry b. constructive c. long d. excited

5. ______ **contraction** of a muscle

a. loosening b. shortening c. firming d. tearing

EXERCISE B: MEANING IN CONTEXT

Use these words to fill in the blanks in the following paragraphs.

structure **reconstruct** **protractor** **traction** **destructive**

After a (1)____________________ windstorm blew down their tree house, Tyrone and Lana decided to (2)____________________ it and make it bigger and better.

"Let's draw the new version before we start building," said Tyrone, pulling out paper and pencil. "I want our new tree house to be an impressive (3)____________________."

"If we put it on the big limb on the right," said Lana, "we'll need to know the angle it makes with the trunk." She pulled out her (4)____________________ to get a general idea of the measure of the angle.

"Not that limb," said Tyrone. "I fell from it last year and broke my leg. At the hospital I was hooked up to cords and weights in (5)____________________ to pull the bone straight so that it would heal well. Let's put the new tree house on a lower limb."

EXERCISE C: EXTEND YOUR VOCABULARY

The "out" prefix: *ex-*, *e-*

In the key word *extract*, the prefix *ex-* means "out." To *extract* a splinter is to pull it out. Match each word that starts with the prefix *ex-* with its meaning.

1. ______ export A. stretch out
2. ______ exit B. ship out
3. ______ extend C. breathe out
4. ______ exhale D. go out

5. Choose two of the words above and write sentences for each.

____

____

____

____

The prefix *ex-* is sometimes spelled *e-*, as in ***emancipate*** meaning "deliver out" or "free." Example: The slaves were *emancipated* in 1863. The prefix *e-* has the same "out" meaning as *ex-*. Match each word that starts with the prefix *e-* with its meaning.

6. _____ erase A. leave out

7. _____ emigrate B. throw out

8. _____ eject C. travel out

9. _____ eliminate D. rub out

10. Choose two of the words above and write sentences for each.

____

____

____

____

LESSON 12

Reviewing Lessons 9–11

EXERCISE A: MATCHING

Match each root with its meaning.

1. ______	civi	A. pull
2. ______	ord	B. build
3. ______	therm	C. measurement
4. ______	metr/meter	D. citizen
5. ______	struct	E. regularity
6. ______	tract	F. heat

In Exercise C of Lessons 9, 10, and 11, you met these prefixes and this suffix. Match the columns.

7. ______	kilo-	G. out
8. ______	milli-	H. noun suffix
9. ______	ex- or e-	I. 1000
10. ______	-ity	J. 1/1000

Write sentences in which you use each of these words meaningfully.

11. extract ____

____

12. kilometer ____

____

13. civility ____

____

EXERCISE B: SORTING

Sort these words, listing each one under its root. When you finish, add another word that goes with each group. (Look back at the lists of familiar and challenge words for ideas.)

contraction	**civil**	**diameter**	**thermal**
civility	**structure**	**civics**	**extraordinary**
extract	**construction**	**traction**	**retract**
geometry	**uncivilized**	**ordinarily**	**destructive**
civilian	**thermostat**	**reconstruct**	**symmetrical**
coordinate	**protractor**	**metronome**	**perimeter**
thermometer			

1. CIVI

____
____
____
____
____
____

2. ORD

____
____
____
____
____
____

3. THERM

____
____
____
____
____
____

4. METR/METER

____
____
____
____
____
____

5. STRUCT

____
____
____
____
____
____

6. TRACT

____
____
____
____
____
____

Write the correct answer in each of the sentences below.

A. Words with the root *struct* are related to the idea of

____.

B. Words with the root *therm* are related to the idea of

____.

C. Words with the root *civi* are related to the idea of

____.

D. The prefixes *kilo-* and *milli-* can be used with the root

____.

E. The meanings of the two parts of the word *thermometer* are

____.

EXERCISE C: VOCABULARY FROM YOUR TEXTBOOKS

Many of the subjects you are studying in school have specific words associated with them. Use these words to answer the following questions.

civics	**contraction**	**protractor**	**metronome**
diameter	**perimeter**	**thermometer**	**geometry**

1. Which word would be most likely to appear in a chapter about weather?

____

2. Which word would be most likely to appear in a lesson about using the apostrophe?

____

3. Which word would be most likely to be in the title of a book about government?

____

4. Which word would you be most likely to hear spoken in music class?

____

5. Which four words would be most likely to appear in a math book?

___________________________ ___________________________

___________________________ ___________________________

EXERCISE D: RHYMING RIDDLES

Write the letter of the answer for each rhyming riddle.

1. ______ What do you call an unruly child who turns up the heat?
2. ______ What do you call the semicircular cover for a tempo clicker?
3. ______ What do you call one third of a cramp?
4. ______ What do you call buying tires that will hug the road?
5. ______ What do you call an exceptional boat for crossing rivers?

A. Traction transaction

B. Thermostat brat

C. Metronome dome

D. Contraction fraction

E. Extraordinary ferry

EXERCISE E: WRITING AND DISCUSSION ACTIVITIES

1. Look at these headlines. Choose one. Then on the lines below, write a paragraph to tell what happened.

   A. Huge Argument between Ordinarily Civil Neighbors

   B. Town Discovers Unusual Thermal Source

   C. Destructive Insects Hold Up Construction

____

____

____

____

2. With a partner, compose a short conversation between one of these pairs of speakers. Make notes for your conversation on the lines below.

   A. A thermostat repairperson and a metronome repairperson, describing the customers who phoned for their help

   B. A civilian nurse and a soldier, discussing the care of their uniforms

   C. A construction worker and a civics teacher, describing their jobs to each other

____

____

3. Look back at the boxes of Challenge Words on pages 37, 38, 41, 42, and 45. From these words, choose three to write on the following lines. Try to define each word.

A. ______________________________

B. ______________________________

C. ______________________________

Now look up those three words in the dictionary. Expand (or revise) your definitions on the following lines.

A. ______________________________

____

B. ______________________________

____

C. ______________________________

____

LESSON 13

Cracking Apart

The roots *frac* as in ***fraction*** and *frag* as in ***fragile*** mean breaking or able to break. The root *rupt* as in ***interrupt*** also means breaking or bursting. In each of the following key words, underline the root.

Key Words

abrupt	fractional	fragility	interruption
disrupt	fracture	fragment	rupture

Using ROOT CLUES

When you spot the root *frac/frag* (break) or the root *rupt* (burst) in a word, you have a key to the word's meaning. Use the underlined root clues to help you match the following columns:

1. _____ fracture — A. a piece that has broken off
2. _____ fragment — B. to break apart
3. _____ interruption — C. to burst open
4. _____ rupture — D. bursting in between two speakers

The root clues did not give you complete definitions as the following dictionary listings will. But they got you started by giving you *part* of the meaning. Sometimes that *part* helps you to figure out the word.

FRAC/FRAG (from the Latin word *fractus/frangere* meaning "to crack; to break")

Familiar Words with Root FRAC/FRAG

- fraction
- fragile

1. fracture (frak′ chər)

n. A break, crack, or split.

After many days of careful work, the sculptor made one wrong tap, causing a fracture in the marble.

v. To break, crack, or split.

When Jabir fractured his arm, he was in a cast for six weeks.

Challenge Words with Root FRAC/FRAG

fracas
infraction
fragmentary

2. fractional (frak′ shən əl)
adj. Having to do with a part, expressed with a numerator and a denominator.

The fractional representation of a half is 1/2.

3. fragility (frə ji′ lə tē)
n. The condition of being easily shattered or broken.

Before the movers arrived, Luz decided to wrap each of the cups separately because of their fragility.

4. fragment (frag′ mənt)
n. A part chipped away, a broken piece.

When I dropped the cup, it broke apart and fragments slid across the floor.

RUPT (from the Latin word *rumpere* meaning "to break; to burst")

Familiar Words with Root RUPT

erupt
interrupt

Challenge Words with Root RUPT

corrupt
incorruptibility

5. abrupt (ə brəpt′)
adj. Sudden, without warning, unexpected.

I had just opened the back door when our dog made an abrupt dash past me to the yard.

6. disrupt (dis rəpt′)
v. To disturb, to break into or destroy orderly progress.

Racing down the street, the howling fire engine disrupted the quiet summer morning.

7. interruption (in tə rəp′ shən)
n. The act of breaking in on.

Mayra could not finish a sentence without an interruption from her talkative friend.

8. rupture (rəp(t)′ shər)
v. To break or burst.

When the pipe ruptured, a column of water shot high into the air.

n. The act of bursting.

The rupture in the gas line forced people to leave the area until it was fixed.

NOTA BENE

Though both *fracture* and *rupture* can mean "break," they convey different kinds of breaking. When a bone breaks, it is called a *fractured* bone. When an appendix breaks open or bursts, it is called a *ruptured* appendix. The two words are used differently: Angry words can cause a *rupture* in a relationship, but not a *fracture.*

EXERCISE A: SYNONYMS

Write the letter of the best SYNONYM (the word or phrase most nearly the same in meaning as the word in bold-faced type).

1. ______ to **fracture** a bone

   a. bruise b. cast c. clean d. crack

2. ______ a small **fragment**

   a. dish b. piece c. split d. cup

3. ______ a serious **rupture**

   a. bursting b. splinter c. injure d. sprain

4. ______ to **disrupt** a game

   a. dissect b. disappoint c. dislike d. disturb

5. ______ an **abrupt** stop

   a. scheduled b. expected c. sudden d. regular

EXERCISE B: MEANING IN CONTEXT

Use these words to fill in the blanks in the following paragraph.

fractional **interruption** **fragments** **disrupt** **fragility**

Students on an archeological dig unearthed (1)________________ of ancient pottery. They needed to handle each piece carefully because of its (2)________________. The students laid everything on a table and began to put the pieces together. They worked for hours without (3)________________. When they stopped, they had assembled only a (4)________________ part of a bowl. Before they left the room, they locked the door so no one would (5)________________ their work.

EXERCISE C: EXTEND YOUR VOCABULARY

The noun suffix *-ment*

One of the key words in this lesson is *fragment.* It has two parts: the root *frag* (break) and the suffix *-ment. Ment* can be used as a suffix on a complete word as well as on a root. Look at the verb *amaze* and the related noun *amazement.*

All of the following words end in *-ment.* Sort them into two groups. On the lines in the first column, write the ones that are a complete word plus the suffix *-ment.* In the second column, write the words in which *-ment* is added to a root.

monument	**amusement**	**ornament**
punishment	**document**	**development**
improvement	**management**	**instrument**
government		

Complete word + *-ment*	**Root + *-ment***
________________	________________
________________	________________
________________	________________
________________	________________
________________	________________
________________	________________

1. What part of speech are all the words in the first column?

   ____

2. On each word in the first column, cross out the suffix *-ment* and look at the base word that is left. What part of speech are all of those words?

   ____

3. On the words in the first column, how does the suffix *-ment* change the original word?

   ____

4. In which column are all the words the names of things you can touch?

   ____

5. What part of speech are all the words in the second column?

   ____

LESSON 14

Placing the Foundation

The root *bas* as in ***basic*** means "foundation, low part." The root *pos* as in ***pose*** means "placement." In each of the following key words, underline the root.

Key Words

basement	bass	dispose	position
basis	composition	exposure	positive

Using ROOT CLUES

The roots *bas* (low) and *pos* (putting or placing) give you clues about meaning. When you spot one of these roots in a word, you know a piece of the word's meaning. Use the underlined clues to help you match the following columns:

1. ______	basement	A. low musical sounds
2. ______	composition	B. placement
3. ______	bass	C. parts put together to make a whole
4. ______	position	D. lowest floor

The root clues did not give you complete definitions as the following dictionary listings will. But they got you started by giving you *part* of the meaning. Sometimes that *part* helps you to figure out the word.

BAS (from the Latin word *bassus* meaning "low," and the Greek word *basis* meaning "pedestal or base")

Familiar Words with Root BAS

- base
- baseboard
- basic

1. basement (bās′ mənt)

n. The lowest floor, partly or fully below the ground.

When the faucet kept dripping, Makayla went to the basement to shut off the water so she could fix the leak.

Challenge Words with Root BAS

- bass drum
- bassoon
- debase

2. basis (bā′ səs)

n. The foundation, the part that supports something.

The basis of my dislike for gossip is that most of it is unkind.

3. bass (bās)

adj. Having deep, low tones.

Since Terrel could sing the low notes, he was placed in the bass section of the chorus.

POS (from the Latin word *positum* meaning "to put, to place")

Familiar Words with Root POS

- pose
- post
- poster
- posture

4. composition (käm′ pə zi shən)

n. 1. The act or the result of making something in writing, art, or music.

The best compositions written by students were posted on the bulletin board.

2. The makeup of a thing, the mixture of parts that make the whole.

The composition of the soil in my yard is fine for growing vegetables, but there's too much shade.

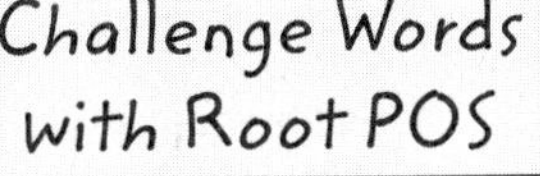

Challenge Words with Root POS

- depose
- impose
- interpose
- proposal
- repose

5. dispose (di spōz′)

v. 1. To get rid of or throw away.

Because of its odor, Ryan disposed of the garbage in a covered container.

2. To take care of or settle.

At our meeting, we disposed of old business first before taking up new items.

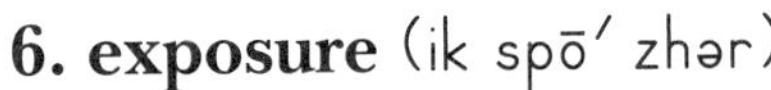

6. exposure (ik spō′ zhər)

n. 1. The result of being unprotected outside, especially in severe weather.

We were worried that the lost hikers would suffer from exposure if we didn't find them soon.

2. The act or result of revealing or putting in open view.

Jenna was embarrassed by the exposure of what she had written in her diary.

7. position (pə zi′ shən)

n. 1. Place or placement.

Alejandro found his position in line, third from the end.

2. Job, rank, office.

Alyssa decided to run for the position of student council president.

3. Point of view, way of thinking.

During the argument over extending the school day, Ms. Garcia stated her position.

8. positive (pä′ zə tiv)

adj. 1. Sure, certain, definite.

The twins were positive that they had left their bicycles in back of the house.

2. Good, favorable, constructive.

Cornel was pleased when the teacher made positive comments about his written report.

EXERCISE A: SYNONYMS

Write the letter of the best SYNONYM (the word or phrase most nearly the same in meaning as the word in bold-faced type).

1. ______ her **position** in the line

a. place b. lead c. posture d. pushing

2. ______ the **basis** of his idea

a. power b. foundation c. construction d. appeal

3. ______ **composition** of the paint

a. odor b. placement c. part d. makeup

4. ______ the **bass** drum

a. chorus b. with low notes c. with high notes d. orchestra

5. ______ hurt by **exposure**

a. being hidden b. being bored c. being revealed d. being punished

EXERCISE B: MEANING IN CONTEXT

Use these words to fill in the blanks in the following paragraph.

positive **position** **basement** **dispose**

When Mom says it's time for spring housecleaning, she means the *whole* house from the attic to the (1)________________. She loves to have everything fresh and clean after the winter. She takes the (2)________________ that everyone in the family should help. Last week she handed me a pail of soapy water. When I frowned, she said, "Look on the (3)________________ side of things; when we're through, we won't need to work this hard until the fall." In addition, she made me clean out my closet and (4)________________ of all the clothes that I'd outgrown. I, too, like everything fresh and organized, but I'll be glad when spring housecleaning is over.

EXERCISE C: EXTEND YOUR VOCABULARY

The noun suffix *-ure*

The key word *exposure* has three meaningful parts: *ex* which can mean "out," *pos* which can mean "put," and *ure* which can mean "the result of being." So, one of the meanings of *exposure* is "the result of being put out (outside)."

Use these words that end in the suffix *-ure* to answer the following questions.

mixture **pleasure** **signature** **rupture** **fracture**

1. Which word can mean the result of signing your name? ________________
2. Which word can mean the result of mixing? ________________
3. Which word can mean the result of being pleased? ________________
4. Which word can mean the result of breaking? ________________
5. Which word can mean the result of bursting? ________________

LESSON 15

Connecting with Prefixes

The prefixes *com-* as in ***com**bine* and *con-* as in ***con**nect* mean "together; with." The prefix *re-* a in ***re**view* means "again; back." In each of the following key words, underline the prefix.

Key Words

committee	conjunction	reaction	reflect
communicate	converse	reelect	relate

Using PREFIX CLUES

The prefixes *com-/con-* (together or with) and *re-* (back or again) give you clues about meaning. When you spot one of these prefixes in a word, you have a key to the word's meaning. Use the underlined prefix clues to help you match the following columns:

1. ______	reelect	A. a group that works together
2. ______	reflect	B. to vote into office again
3. ______	committee	C. to think back about
4. ______	converse	D. to talk with

The prefix clues did not give you complete definitions as the following dictionary listings will. But they got you started by giving you *part* of the meaning. Sometimes that *part* helps you to figure out the word.

COM-/CON- (from the Latin word *cum* meaning "together, with")

Familiar Words with Prefixes COM-/CON

- combine
- commotion
- compare
- conductor
- congress
- connection

Challenge Words with Prefixes COM-/CON

- compete
- condone
- congestion
- contrite

1. committee (kə mi′ tē)
n. A group of people who work together on some matter.

The students on the planning committee for the science fair came up with a schedule for the event.

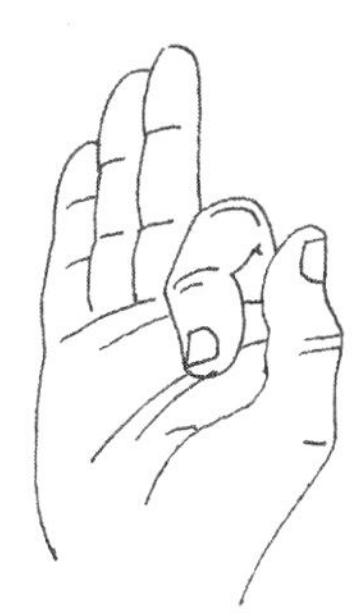

2. communicate (kə myü′ nə kāt)
v. To make known, to share information together.

Zaida learned sign language so that she could communicate with her cousin who could not hear.

communication, n.

3. converse (kän vərs′)
v. To talk together.

Both boys were talkative, so they liked to converse every time they got together.

conversation, n.

4. conjunction (kən jənk′ shən) [also derived from Latin *jungere* meaning "to join"]
n. 1. A joining word; the part of speech that joins other words or groups of words.

In the sentence, "Kim and Lee liked baseball, but not tennis," the words *and* and *but* are conjunctions.

2. A joining together.

Volunteers worked in conjunction with scientists to help the beached whales.

RE- (from Latin meaning "back or again")

Familiar Words with Prefix RE-
rearrange
recall
repeat
return
review
rewrite

Challenge Words with Prefix RE-
refute
remit
repose

5. reaction (rē ak′ shən)

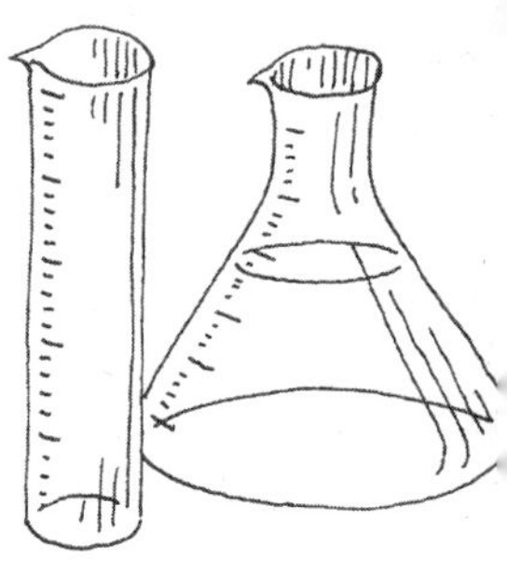

n. 1. A response.

When my little brother hears "No," his reaction is to cry.

2. The production of a chemical change in substances.

During chemical reactions, new products with different properties are formed.

6. reelect (rē ə lekt′)

v. To vote into office for another term; to chose and elect again.

After serving one term as class representative to the student counci Dwayne was reelected.

reelection, n.

7. reflect (ri flekt′) [also derived from Latin *flectere* meaning "to bend")

v. 1. To bend or throw back light, heat, or sound.

The surface of the lake was so smooth that, looking down, I could see my face reflected as if from a mirror.

2. To think back about; to consider carefully.

Reflecting on the events of the day, Kalila knew she would not have changed a single thing.

reflection, n.

8. relate (ri lāt′)

v. 1. To have a connection with.

Often the meaning of a word is related to, and can be traced back to, its root.

2. To tell.

Over the dinner table, Sidone related how well her team had played in the soccer tournament.

EXERCISE A: SYNONYMS

Write the letter of the best SYNONYM (the word or phrase most nearly the same in meaning as the word in bold-faced type).

1. ______ using a **conjunction** in the sentence

   a. noun b. verb c. group d. joining word

2. ______ to **relate** to

   a. be done b. connect c. bend d. repeat

3. ______ **reelect** the president

   a. side with b. campaign c. vote d. choose again

4. ______ **communicate** information

   a. make known b. decide on c. join d. hide

5. ______ to **reflect** upon

   a. dream b. judge c. consider d. serve

EXERCISE B: MEANING IN CONTEXT

Use these words to fill in the blanks in the following paragraphs.

related **Committee** **reaction** **conversed** **reelected**

Each member of the Science Fair (1)________________ had a different idea about how to arrange the displays. Danya, who had attended last year's fair, (2)________________ how several projects got broken when people bumped into the tables. Jason and Allison became irritated with each other when they (3)________________ about where to put the tables. Soon they were having an argument. When Zoe, the chairperson, tried to get them to cooperate, their (4)________________ was to argue with her, too. Although she finally restored order, Zoe hoped she would not be (5)________________ to the committee when the science fair came around next year.

EXERCISE C: EXTEND YOUR VOCABULARY

Other spellings of "with" prefix *com-/con-*: *col-*, *co-*, *cor-*

The prefix *com-/con-* (together, with) is sometimes spelled other ways. Look at *col-* in *collect* (to gather *together*). Look at *co-* in *cooperate* (to work *with*). Look at *cor-* in *correspond* (to communicate *with* by letters). All these spellings of the prefix carry the meaning "together, with."

Sort these words according to the spelling of the prefix by listing each one under COM-, CON-, or OTHER.

concert	**community**
collision	**congruent**
companion	**connection**
collage	**coordinate**
correspondence	**company**

COM-	**CON-**	**OTHER**
________	________	________
________	________	________
________	________	________
________	________	________

1. Which word means "an event where people hear music *together*"?

____

2. Which word means "a work of art made by putting *together* a variety of things"?

____

3. Which word means "a bumping *together* of two cars"?

____

4. Which word means "a joining *with*"?

____

5. Which word means "a person *with* whom you are friendly"?

____

6. What meaning is shared by these prefixes: *com-, con-, col-, co-, cor-*?

____

Reviewing Lessons 13–15

EXERCISE A: MATCHING

Match each root or prefix with its meaning.

1. ______ com-/con- A. burst
2. ______ rupt B. break
3. ______ re- C. together; with
4. ______ frac/frag D. again
5. ______ bas E. place
6. ______ pos F. low

Write sentences in which you use each of these words meaningfully.

7. reelection ______________________________

____

8. mixture ______________________________

____

9. fragility ______________________________

____

10. conversation ______________________________

____

11. signature ______________________________

____

EXERCISE B: SORTING

Sort these words, listing each one under its root or prefix. When you finish, add another wo that goes with each group. (Look back at the list of familiar and challenge words for ideas.)

committee	**reflect**	**reelect**	**positive**
position	**fracture**	**abrupt**	**fragility**
composition	**basement**	**basis**	**disrupt**
relate	**communicate**	**rupture**	**fragment**
fractional	**exposure**	**bass**	**converse**
interruption	**dispose**	**conjunction**	**reaction**

1. FRAC/FRAG

______

______

______

______

______

______

2. RUPT

______

______

______

______

______

______

3. POS

______

______

______

______

______

______

4. BAS

______

______

______

______

______

______

5. COM-/CON-

______

______

______

______

______

______

6. RE-

______

______

______

______

______

______

Write the answers for these questions.

A. Which column contains words with a prefix that can mean "with"? ______

B. Which column contains words with a prefix that can mean "back"? ______

C. Which word could be listed in two columns? ______

D. What are the meanings of the two parts of the word *rupture*? ______

EXERCISE C: VOCABULARY FROM YOUR TEXTBOOKS

Many of the subjects you are studying in school have specific words associated with them. Use these words to answer the following questions.

fragility **bass** **fracture** **reelect** **fractional**

1. Which word would be most likely to appear in a music lesson?

______

2. As you read a lesson on first aid, which word will you probably see?

______

3. As you study the history of voting in the United States, which word might you read?

______

4. When you read about objects found in Egyptian pyramids, which word might you see?

______

5. As you work on math problems, which word would be most likely to appear?

______

EXERCISE D: RHYMING RIDDLES

Write the letter of the answer for each rhyming riddle.

1. ______ What do you call a place for talking?
2. ______ What do you call the job done by a joining word?
3. ______ What do you call fixing a mistake in counting votes?
4. ______ What do you call thinking about which way to turn?
5. ______ What do you call feeling bad after having a tooth pulled?
6. ______ What do you call a group of people working for the betterment of urban ca

A. City kitty committee

B. Election correction

C. Conjunction function

D. Extraction reaction

E. Communication station

F. Direction reflection

EXERCISE E: WRITING AND DISCUSSION ACTIVITIES

1. Look at these headlines. Choose one. Then on the lines below, write a paragraph to tell what happened.

   A. Ruptured Water Pipe May Bring Positive Result

   B. Fragments of Rare Old Instrument Discovered in Basement

   C. Disposing of Old Toys Creates New Problem

____

____

____

____

2. With a partner, compose a conversation between one of these pairs of speakers. Make notes for your conversation on the lines below.

   A. A student who reflects before speaking and a student who blurts things out abruptly

   B. A storyteller who hates to be interrupted and a "class clown" who loves to create disruptions

   ___

   ___

3. Look back at the boxes of Challenge Words on pages 55, 59, 63, and 64. From these words, choose three to write on the following lines. Try to define each word.

   A. ___

   B. ___

   C. ___

Now look up these three words in the dictionary. Expand (or revise) your definitions on the following lines.

A. ___

___

B. ___

___

C. ___

___

WORD LIST

(Numbers in parentheses refer to the lesson in which the word appears.)

abrupt (13)
aquaculture (5)
aquamarine (5)
aquatic (5)
astronaut (6)
astronomical (6)
astronomy (6)

basement (14)
basis (14)
bass (14)

circuit (1)
circular (1)
circulate (1)
civics (9)
civil (9)
civilian (9)
civility (9)
committee (15)
communicate (15)
composition (14)
conjunction (15)
construction (11)
contraction (11)
converse (15)
coordinate (9)
cycle (1)
cyclone (1)

dependent (2)
destructive (11)
diameter (10)
dispose (14)
disrupt (13)

equality (2)
equate (2)
equator (2)
equidistant (2)
equilateral (2)
exposure (14)
extract (11)
extraordinary (9)

fractional (13)
fracture (13)
fragility (13)
fragment (13)

geometry (10)

inactive (7)
informal (7)
insignificant (7)
insomnia (7)
interactive (3)
interfere (3)
intermittent (3)
interruption (13)
intersect (3)
interval (3)

Mediterranean (5)
metronome (10)

ordinarily (9)

pending (2)
pendulum (2)
perimeter (10)
position (14)
positive (14)
protractor (11)

reaction (15)
reconstruct (11)
recycle (1)
reelect (15)
reflect (15)
relate (15)
retract (11)
rupture (13)

semiannual (7)
semicircle (1)
semicolon (7)
semiconscious (7)
semiformal (7)
semiprecious (7)
structure (11)
subterranean (5)
symmetrical (10)

telecast (6)
teleconference (6)
telegraph (6)
telemarketing (6)
telescope (6)
terrace (5)
terrain (5)
territory (5)
thermal (10)
thermometer (10)
thermostat (10)
traction (11)
transact (3)
transfer (3)
transfusion (3)
transmit (3)

uncivilized (9)
unicycle (1)